FAMOUS PEOPLE
FAMOUS LIVES

Biographies of famous people
to support the curriculum.

Wolfgang Amadeus Mozart

by Harriet Castor

Illustrations by Peter Kent

W

FRANKLIN WATTS

NEW YORK • LONDON • SYDNEY

First published in 1997 by
Franklin Watts
96 Leonard Street
London
EC2A 4RH

Franklin Watts Australia
14 Mars Road
Lane Cove
NSW 2066

This edition 1999

ISBN: 0 7496 2607 0

A CIP catalogue record for this book
is available from the British Library.

Dewey Decimal Classification Number: 780.92

10 9 8 7 6 5 4 3 2

Series editor: Sarah Ridley
Designer: Kirstie Billingham
Consultant: Dr Anne Millard

Printed in Great Britain

Wolfgang Amadeus Mozart

The Mozart family lived in
Austria. Leopold Mozart was
a musician and composer. His
little daughter, Nannerl, played
the harpsichord brilliantly.
Then in 1756 a new Mozart
was born.

Wolfgang Amadeus Mozart was a small pale child, but he quickly showed he had a talent even more amazing than his sister's. At four, he could play pieces from Nannerl's music book – and soon afterwards he started composing his own music.

His father believed this talent was
a gift from God.

Before long Wolfgang could play the harpsichord as well as a grown-up musician. But that wasn't all.

When he was seven he played an organ for the first time – just as if he'd been practising for months.

He picked up a violin, too,
and played perfectly – without
a single lesson!

Leopold knew his children were so amazing that people would pay to see them play. So he took them on tours all round Europe. They even played for Empress Maria Theresa of Austria.

What a clever child!

Little Wolfgang loved playing,
but the tours were hard work.
He sometimes felt homesick, too.
Wolfgang and his father
carried on touring right through
his childhood.

At that time music was very important in Austria. Everyone who could afford lessons learnt how to play an instrument.

Rich people even kept their own private orchestras, so that they could put on concerts and operas and grand dances. The Emperor was particularly fond of music.

But professional musicians
were not respected. Many
people thought they were
uneducated, and just another
type of servant.

12

When Mozart grew up he got a
job working for the Archbishop
of Salzburg. He had to eat at the
servants' table and he didn't like
it one bit!

Mozart was confident and headstrong. The Archbishop thought he was far too proud.

They had a row and Mozart was so rude to the Archbishop that everyone was shocked. The Archbishop was furious. Mozart was thrown out of the room and kicked down the stairs.

Meanwhile Mozart had fallen
in love with a young woman
called Constanze Weber. They
were married in the cathedral
in Vienna.

Mozart's father didn't approve
of Constanze, but Mozart
adored her. They were to have
six children, although only
two survived.

Now Mozart was living in Vienna and had become very popular there. He conducted and played in concerts of his own music. He gave piano lessons to rich pupils, too.

Lots of people bought copies of his music to play themselves.

Mozart and Constanze had plenty of money. They moved into a large apartment.

Mozart was very busy. Luckily, he could compose at any time, anywhere. He jotted down ideas when he was on horseback, or having his hair done, or in the middle of a game of billiards.

He could write very quickly, too.
He once wrote a whole
symphony in just five days.
And it was beautiful!

People were amazed when they saw Mozart's manuscripts – he never made mistakes or corrections. He finished everything perfectly in his head before he wrote it down.

This was very useful. Mozart
was messy, and was always
losing pages of his music. But
when a page went missing, he
simply wrote it out again. He
never forgot a single note.

Though Mozart's music was beautiful and often serious, he had a great sense of humour. He was friends with another famous composer, Joseph Haydn, and they both loved practical jokes and parties.

My dear Mozart!

Mozart wrote a lot of letters to his friends and family. They were often full of jokes – and rude ones, too!

Sometimes Mozart's sense of humour was put to use in his work. He was brilliant at writing comic operas. He created wonderful characters and splendid theatrical effects through his music.

Two of his best-known comic operas are 'The Marriage of Figaro' and 'The Magic Flute'.

But Mozart couldn't just compose whatever he wanted. To earn money, he needed to write music people liked to listen to and play.

Musical clocks were very popular at this time. Mozart thought they were nasty, squeaky things, but he still composed music for them. He would have preferred to write more church music instead.

Mozart could even do musical impressions – and this helped him to help a friend.

The friend was a composer, and he was ill. He had to finish a piece of music or he would lose his job. So Mozart secretly wrote it for him. Mozart did such a good impression of his friend's style that no one suspected the truth!

Mozart didn't spend all his time in Vienna. He went to Prague, for instance, several times. One of his most famous operas, 'Don Giovanni', was written for an opera company there.

When 'The Marriage of Figaro' was performed in Prague, Mozart said that all around the city he could hear people whistling tunes from it.

Mozart composed many different types of music: operas, symphonies, concertos ... music for piano, strings, wind instruments ... dance music, church music – the list is a long one!

Incredibly, it was all beautiful music – even the pieces he composed in a hurry. No wonder other composers were jealous.

However, composers then were rather like pop stars – they were popular one minute, and unpopular the next.

The same music might do well in one city but not in another. Prague loved 'Don Giovanni', but Vienna wasn't so sure. Mozart's opera 'Idomeneo' was hardly performed during his lifetime. Now it is very famous.

The philistines! They've cancelled my opera.
LA CLEMENZA DI TITO
DRAMMA SERIO PER MUSICA
W A MOZART
NEL TEAT
ALE

By the time Mozart was thirty-one, he wasn't so popular in Vienna any more. Some people said his music was too difficult. Austria was at war, too, and many nobles cut down their spending on music.

Perhaps my friends can lend me some money.

Constanze fell ill, and her
treatments were expensive.
Mozart slid into debt.

We'll have to move into
a smaller apartment.

In 1791, though, Mozart's fortunes revived. His dance music was popular again, and he received an anonymous message asking him to write a Requiem (music for a funeral).

He found a new job, too, at the cathedral. He was excited; he would be able to pay his debts and write more church music.

But Mozart began to feel unwell.

41

Mozart worked hard on the Requiem. He felt so ill he started thinking it was for his own funeral.

The Requiem never got finished
– but Mozart carried on
composing right until he died.
Instead of last words he made
last sounds: trying to show what
he wanted the drums to play.

Mozart was just thirty-five when he died. He hadn't had time to take up his cathedral job, and he left so little money that he had to be buried in an unmarked grave.

Yet his fame lived on and grew. Today Mozart's music is loved by millions of people, and is played all over the world.

Further facts

Peculiar pianos

Mozart wrote
lots of music
for the piano.
But the piano
in Mozart's time
was a new invention,
and it was rather different from the
modern instrument. Some pianos
then had pedals you operated with
your knees.

Was Mozart murdered?

An old rival and enemy of Mozart's,
called Salieri, claimed later that he
had poisoned Mozart. Mozart himself,
during his final illness, suspected it

was poisoning. But, from the evidence we still have of his symptoms, this seems unlikely.

Mozart in code

Wolfgang and his father wrote to each other a great deal. They worried that the authorities might open and read their letters, so they often wrote in code. One favourite trick was to call themselves 'Trazom'. Can you work out why?

Some important dates in Wolfgang Amadeus Mozart's lifetime

1756 Mozart is born in Salzburg, Austria.

1761 Aged five, Mozart plays in public for the first time.

1762 Mozart's father takes him and his sister, Nannerl, on their first tour.

1779 The Archbishop of Salzburg employs Mozart as court organist.

1781 Mozart leaves the Archbishop's service and settles in Vienna.

1782 Mozart marries Constanze Weber in St Stephen's Cathedral, Vienna.

1787 Mozart writes 'Don Giovanni' and conducts the first performance in Prague.

1787 Mozart's popularity in Vienna wanes. He slides into debt.

1791 Mozart is popular in Vienna again. He is asked to write a Requiem and gets a job at the cathedral.

1791 December, Mozart dies aged thirty-five, leaving the Requiem unfinished.